READING CHAMPION

GERDA'S JOURNEY

by Katie Woolley and James Croft

W
FRANKLIN WATTS
LONDON•SYDNEY

Once upon a time, a magic mirror broke into a million pieces.
The pieces flew all around the world.
If a piece went into someone's eye, they would only see the bad in people.

One day, a piece of the mirror flew into the eye of Gerda's friend, Kay.

Dear Diary,

Something is the matter with Kay.
He used to be my best friend,
but now he doesn't want to play with
me anymore. He looks sad all the time.
I don't know what to do.
I am so worried about him.

Gerda

Dear Diary,

I can't find Kay anywhere!
I've asked all the villagers,
but no one has seen him.
I'm worried that something bad
has happened to him.
I'm going to look for him.
Maybe he went down to the river.
It is his favourite place.

Gerda

Dear Diary,

I went down to the river today. Kay wasn't there, but I did meet a talking bird. The bird told me that Kay was taken by the Snow Queen. It said I must go to her palace to rescue Kay.

Wish me luck on my journey.

Gerda

Dear Diary,

I've been walking for seven days and seven nights. It's getting colder and colder the further north I go. There is snow all around me, but I will keep going until I find Kay.

Gerda

Dear Diary,

I am so cold but, at last, I have found the Snow Queen's palace.
I was walking through a snow storm when I saw some beautiful blue lights.
I looked up and saw a huge palace on top of a mountain.
Kay must be inside.
I'm going there tomorrow.

Gerda

Dear Diary,

I have found Kay! I was near the Snow Queen's palace when I saw him!
He was in the middle of a frozen lake.
He looked so cold and lonely.
I thought he had been turned into an ice statue so I started to cry.

My tears went onto his face and it started to turn warm and pink.
Then, Kay started to cry too!
When he wiped away his tears, a piece of magic glass fell out of his eye.

Suddenly, Kay could remember everything again!

Gerda

Dear Diary,

Kay and I got back home yesterday.
We couldn't wait to tell everyone about our snowy adventure and warn the villagers to look out for magic glass.
I hope we never see another piece of that glass ever again.
How lucky I am to have found my friend!

Gerda

Story order

Look at these 5 pictures and captions.
Put the pictures in the right order
to retell the story.

1

Gerda found Kay on a lake.

2

Magic glass went into Kay's eye.

3

The magic glass fell out of Kay's eye.

4

Kay didn't want to play with Gerda.

5

Gerda went to look for Kay.

Independent Reading

This series is designed to provide an opportunity for your child to read on their own. These notes are written for you to help your child choose a book and to read it independently.

In school, your child's teacher will often be using reading books which have been banded to support the process of learning to read. Use the book band colour your child is reading in school to help you make a good choice. *Gerda's Journey* is a good choice for children reading at Gold Band in their classroom to read independently. The aim of independent reading is to read this book with ease, so that your child enjoys the story and relates it to their own experiences.

About the book

When a piece of magic glass goes into Kay's eye, he doesn't want to be Gerda's friend anymore. Then he disappears! Gerda is determined to find her friend, and she goes on a long journey ...

Before reading

Help your child to learn how to make good choices by asking: "Why did you choose this book? Why do you think you will enjoy it?" Look at the cover together and ask: "What do you think the story will be about?" Support your child to think of what they already know about the story context. Read the title aloud and remind your child of the story of *The Snow Queen*. Ask: "Do you remember who Gerda is?" Explain that Gerda is Kay's best friend. Remind your child that they can try to sound out the letters to make a word if they get stuck.

Decide together whether your child will read the story independently or read it aloud to you.

During reading

If reading aloud, support your child if they hesitate or ask for help by telling them the word. Remind your child of what they know and what they can do independently. If reading to themselves, remind your child that they can come and ask for your help if stuck.

After reading

Support comprehension by asking your child to tell you about the story. Use the story order puzzle to encourage your child to retell the story in the right sequence, in their own words. The correct sequence can be found on the next page.
Give your child a chance to respond to the story: "Did you have a favourite part? Did you expect Gerda to find Kay at the end of the story?"
Help your child think about the messages in the book that go beyond the story and ask: "Why do you think Gerda went looking for Kay, even when he wasn't nice to her?"

Extending learning

Think about the story with your child, and make comparisons with the story *The Snow Queen*. Help your child understand the story structure by using the same story context and adding different elements. "Let's make up a new story about Gerda and Kay at the Snow Queen's palace. What happens in your story?"
In the classroom, your child's teacher may be looking at fronted adverbial phrases to add information to sentences. On a few of the pages, look at some of these with your child, such as: Once upon a time; One day; When he wiped away his tears; Suddenly.

Franklin Watts
First published in Great Britain in 2024
by Hodder and Stoughton

Series Editors: Jackie Hamley and Melanie Palmer
Series Advisors and Development Editors: Dr Sue Bodman and Glen Franklin
Series Designers: Cathryn Gilbert and Peter Scoulding

A CIP catalogue record for this book is
available from the British Library.

ISBN 978 1 4451 9109 6 (hbk)
ISBN 978 1 4451 9111 9 (pbk)
ISBN 978 1 4451 9110 2 (ebook)

Printed in China

Franklin Watts
An imprint of
Hachette Children's Group
Part of Hodder and Stoughton
Carmelite House
50 Victoria Embankment
London EC4Y 0DZ

An Hachette UK Company
www.hachette.co.uk

www.reading-champion.co.uk

FSC
www.fsc.org
MIX
Paper | Supporting
responsible forestry
FSC® C104740

Story order: 2, 4, 5, 1, 3